JOKES FOR
YOUR JOHN

Jokes for your John

Written by: Omri Bar Lev
Illustrated by: Joe Weis

Barricade Books Inc.
New York

Published by Barricade Books Inc.
150 Fifth Avenue
New York, NY 10011

Printed in the United States of America.

Library of Congress Cataloging-in-Publication Data

Barlev, Omri
        Jokes for your john : the full bathroom reader / by Omri Barlev/
    and Joe Weis.
        p.   cm.
    ISBN 1-56980-063-4
    1. Toilets--Humor.   I. Weis, Joe, II. Title.
PN6231.W3B37   1996
818'.5402--dc20   95-51072
                                                            CIP

First printing

FIRST
MOVEMENT

THANK YOU

I'd like to thank… no one, actually. Don't anyone even think about asking for a cut of my royalties, either. But as long as there's already a Thank You section, I might as well thank my grandmother. If she hadn't left Russia sixty-five years ago, I would probably have been writing from a Gulag asking for a pardon instead of writing this book.

Also, grudging thanks to the three people who showed up by mistake at my last birthday party, and to my friends, who spend most of their time trying to figure out how I've managed to make money from jokes that aren't funny.

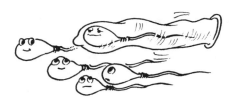

WARNING

This book is definitely not intended to be read anywhere near teachers, including my high school comp teacher who gave me a C- on my report card. Looking back, she was right.

This book should also not be read in the presence of my tax consultant, whose good mood is enough to spoil my best day; bank clerks with glasses; people more talented that I am; and, of course, all lawyers, doctors, psychoanalysts and all those who make money off other people's problems.

"Hi, Superman, where have you been?" the wife asks her husband.
"At work, of course," replies the man.
"How come you smell so nice, Superman?" she continues.
"There was a meeting. I dropped a pen and my secretary and I bent over to pick it up at the same time. I guess you smell her perfume."
"And the lipstick on your collar, Superman?"
"As we bent over, her lips must have accidently brushed my collar."
"And the loose button, Superman?"
"Oh, that. The shirt got caught on the corner of the table when I picked up the pen – the button must've come loose. But why do you keep calling me Superman?"
"Well, only Superman wears his underwear over his pants…"

Once the engagement ring was on her finger she turned to her fiancé and said: "After we're married, sweetie, we'll have three children."
"How do you know?" he asked.
"Cause right now they're at my mother's."

I'm going for a walk, wait here for me …

A honeymooning couple arrive at the hotel to find that the room has separate beds. They turn out the light, and the husband calls his wife to his bed. In the dark she bangs her foot on the night table between the two beds.

"Does it hurt, sweetheart?" says her mate, gently kissing her foot. "I'll make it feel all better."

After they make love the wife goes back to her bed and bangs her foot again.

"Can't you watch where you're going, you clumsy cow?"

Joe, who had a reputation, was going on a date. His friends told him to be good and not to mention screwing or blowjobs right away. Joe promised to behave.

In the middle of the movie he can contain himself no longer. "May I put my arm around you?" he asks gently.

"Absolutely not!" was the reply.

"Then I guess I shouldn't ask you about a fuck after the movie..."

Excited, Bill calls his wife: "Mary, pack the suitcases right away!"

"Why, what's happened?" she asks.

"I won a million bucks in the lottery!" Bill replies.

"Wonderful!" says Mary, "Where are we going?"

"We're not going anywhere. You're leaving!"

"**Y**ou know, Daddy, the milkman has a new pecker," says little Jenny.
"How do you know?" asks her astonished father.
"Because today I saw him showing it to mummy, and it was still wrapped up."

Coming for the
Therapist
The advice column of Dr. P. Anus

Q: Lately my wife complains of headaches. Could it be a side effect from her meeting with my sledge hammer, or is she faking it so she won't have to have sex with me?

O.J.
Los Angeles, California

A: Dear J. Does the J stand for Jason? You neglected to tell me whether her headache is accompanied by a black eye, a flattened forehead, missing teeth and broken vertebra. Without this information, it's hard for me to diagnose.

A woman to her maid: "My husband is cheating on me with another woman."
"You're only saying that to make me jealous!" answers the maid.

On a gravestone:
Here lies my darling wife, Murielle. Alone at last…

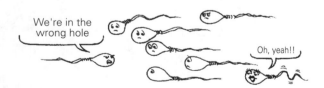

Mr. and Mrs. Brown are in bed when suddenly the phone rings. Mr. Brown picks it up. A voice says, "This is the Boston Strangler."
He hands to his wife, saying, "It's for you…"

A woman is in bed with a naive young man. To put him at his ease she engages him in small talk.

"You know," she begins, "I think women who swim have broad shoulders."

The man murmurs softly.

"And do you know that women who play tennis have large hands?" she continues.

Again the only sound is a slight murmur. After a few moments he says, "Is it true you're an avid horsewoman?"

Sweetie – no condom – no way!!!

...AND DILDO DONNA SAYS:
"I don't do it with just anyone – only those who want to!"

Bill is about to screw his wife when a mouse sneaks between her legs into her pussy. Bill immediately calls the doctor and tells him about it.
"No worries," says the doctor, "I'll be there in ten minutes. Until I get there put a piece of cheese between your wife's legs. When the mouse comes out to eat the cheese, catch it."
Ten minutes later, the doctor arrives. Bill has a fish between his wife's legs.
"In heaven's name, what are you doing?" shouts the doctor. "I specifically said cheese!"
"Well doc, till you got here, the cat went in."

What do National Geographic and Playboy have in common?
They both show places you'll never get to.

See you in the.. s..e..w..e..r ...

Two guys are standing in the street when one of them notices a dog licking its balls.
"Jeez" says one, "I wish I could do that!"
"Look," says the other, "you should probably get to know him better first."

An Australian sheep farmer was in dire straits when his sheep couldn't concieve. He consulted the vet.

"Yes," said the vet, "this is a well-known problem. Sometimes the passages in sheep are either very tight or closed and conception is impossible. You must to open up their passages yourself. In other words, you have to screw them."

"How will I know if it works?" asked the farmer.

"Very simply," replied the doctor, "on the morning after you 'help' them, check them. If the sheep are on the top of the hill, they are pregnant. If they are at the bottom, they're not."

The farmer went home. The next morning he got up early, loaded the sheep on his truck and drove behind the hill so that no one would see him. In the evening, after screwing the whole herd, he loaded them back on the truck and went home.

As soon as the sun was up, he went to the window to check the sheeps' location, and saw that they were all at the bottom of the hill. He quickly phoned the doctor and told him what had happened.

"This also happens sometimes," said the doctor, "sometimes once is not enough. You have to do it again."

Having no other choice, the farmer again got up early, loaded the sheep on the truck, drove around the hill, unloaded them, and screwed them again. After he was done with the whole herd he loaded them back on the truck and went home, completely exhausted. In the morning he got up casually and peeped out the window. His entire herd was still at the bottom of the hill! In desperation he phoned the vet again.

"Listen," said the vet, "there is another option, but it's very expensive. I suggest that before resorting to it you screw your sheep one last time."

With no energy or desire whatsoever, the farmer agreed to do it one last time. On the following morning, he got up, loaded the sheep on the truck, drove around the hill, did his deed, barely getting through the last sheep in the herd. Finally, at dusk he loaded the sheep back on the truck, drove home, unloaded the sheep and crawled into bed. Sleep overcame him immediately.

In the morning the farmer woke up but couldn't move. He called his wife and said: "I can't move, so could you please look out the window and tell me whether the sheep are at the top or the bottom of the hill?" The wife went over to the window and looked outside. She turned to her husband and said "That's funny, they're neither at the top or the bottom of the hill... they're all on the truck, and some are honking the horn..."

Paul paid for his son to take violin lessons. One day the son offers to play for his father. He picks up the violin and as soon as he starts playing, the father gets an erection. Amazed, he calls his friend Joe and tells him what has happened, and asks him if he has an explanation.

"Sure," says he, "It's really very simple. The boy plays like a fucking cunt!"

Stop shoving back there

"Doc, my tits droop. What can I do to perk them up?"
"Walk on all fours."

A man with a stammer goes to the doctor. The doctor tells him to undress.

After examining the naked man carefully, the doctor makes his diagnosis.

"To cure you, I must chop off a small piece of your penis." He does so, and to the man's amazement, the stammer disappears.

A week later the man comes back to the doctor:

"I want you to replace the piece you chopped off. My wife says she doesn't mind the stammer so much if I get my natural size back."

"S-s-so-sorry, b-b-b-but I-I-I ca-ca-can't."

This guy was spending a rainy afternoon with a married woman. Suddenly she cries out: "Hurry, hurry, my husband is coming. Quick, jump out the window."

The guy, not taking any chances, doesn't get dressed and jumps naked into the street. As luck would have it, he lands right in the middle of a marathon run. Being in good shape he falls in stride with the others. One of the runners turns to him and says,

"Excuse me, do you always run like this?"

"Yes, it's nice and comfortable to run naked."

"Yes, but with a condom?"

"Oh… only when it's raining…"

A fisherman sits on the bank, daydreaming happily. All of a sudden, a kid appears and grabs a frog that had been hopping along the bank. He takes out a pocketknife and says to the frog, "I could cut your legs off, and then slit your gut… "

"Listen, kid," says the fisherman, "Whatever you do to that frog I'll do to you!"

"However," continues the kid, "today's your lucky day. I'm going to kiss your ass."

A woman goes to her gynecologist because she can't get her vibrator out. After examining her thoroughly, he tells her: "There's good news and bad news. The bad news is that I can't get the vibrator out. The good news is that I replaced the batteries."

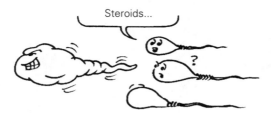

A gynecologist is examining a woman. He has his right hand in her vagina when the phone rings. He picks up the receiver with his left – on the line is another patient asking for directions to the clinic.
The doctor starts to give directions, while his right hand, still in the woman's vagina, moves accordingly – once to the right, then to the left and to the left again.
As he puts down the receiver, the woman says, "Doctor, couldn't you have your clinic a little farther out of town?"

Little Joseph couldn't control his mouth. Whenever he went for a walk with Mommy he would make lascivious comments about all the women he saw. His mother, sick of hearing Joseph's impolite comments, sent him to school in a monastery. Three years later Joseph came home. He and his father got on a bus to visit Grandma.

"Wow, son, look at that hot chick!" said Dad.

Joseph, looking around, replied: "Aw Dad, she's nothing compared with the driver…"

Johnny comes home and hears moaning from his mother's bedroom. Carefully, he looks through the keyhole and sees Mommy masturbating, groaning, "I want a man, I want a man..."
The following day, when he comes home he again hears groaning, and checks his mother's room. A strange man is in bed with her.
A couple of days later his mother comes home. She hears groans coming from Johnny's room and goes to check. There is Johnny, rubbing his little pecker and moaning: "Bicycle, bicycle..."

What is a woman's best friend?
A man's imagination.

Two fleas meet. One of them has a very bad cold and can't stop sneezing.
"How did you get such a nasty cold?" asks his friend.
"I hitched a ride from New York to Florida on a biker's moustache, and I must have caught cold from the breeze."
"Do what I do," says his buddy, "next time, hitch with a stewardess – snuggle in her pubic hair and you'll be warm and cozy – and you won't catch cold."
A week later they meet again, but the flea's cold is worse than before.
"Why didn't you do as I suggested?"
"I did," says our flea, "I found a nice warm spot in a stewardess's pussy but after about an hour I was on the biker's moustache again."

BONER: "After I come, I go!"

A Native American boy asks his dad: "Father, why do Americans have short names like Joe, Ben or Sam while we all have long ones?"
"It's simple," says the father, "We name our children after an event that happened before their birth. For instance, High Mountain got his name because he was born on a high mountain. Do you understand, Hole In Rubber?"

I hope you're not one of those who fuck and fly...

A professor doing research on insanity was interviewing a hospitalized patient. "What made you crazy?" asked the professor.
"Well," began the patient, "I was screwing this married woman. Just as I got undressed her husband came home. I jumped out the window and held on to the ledge. It took him only a few seconds to find me and he started hitting my hands, first with his hand and then with his shoe. I managed to hold on, and then he stuffed some paper between my fingers and set my hands on fire."
"Is this when you lost it?" asked the excited professor.
"No," answered the patient, "it happened when I looked down and saw three feet between me and the ground."

Little Red Riding Hood is strolling in the forest when suddenly she spots a wolf sitting by a tree.
"Big Bad Wolf," she says to him, "Why are your eyes so big?"
"Get out of here, you stupid bitch, and let me shit in peace!"

A horny mouse wanders through the forest. He sees a female elephant under a tree. Quickly he climbs her from behind and puts his tool in her. Just then a coconut falls from the tree right on the elephant's head.
"Aoowww!!" she screams.
Breathless, the mouse says, "Suffer, baby, suffer..."

Screaming and yelling, an old woman enters a police station : "I'm here to lodge a complaint. A few moments ago a virgin young man tried to rape me."
"Excuse me, ma'am, but just how do you know he was a virgin?"
"Because I had to show him how."

A researcher is caught by a gorilla while on safari in Africa. The gorilla ties him to a tree and rapes him constantly for a month. Finally he is rescued by a friend. Two months later, they meet in the street and it is obvious that the researcher is really down.
"Let it go," says the friend, "snap out of it. It's been two months now."
"How can I snap out of it," replies the researcher, "she doesn't write or call, nothing…"

A family of rabbits is blessed with another bunny – all white, except for a small black triangle on his ear.
Because of this little deformity his brothers and friends reject him and bully him around. When he can no longer take the abuse, he decides to get rid of the ear with the black triangle. He goes over to the railroad track, puts his ear on the tracks and waits for the train. It comes roaring by, completely mangling the bunny.
Moral: Don't lose your head over a small black triangle.

What would you like to drink before you go home?

Three men are discussing the size of their wive's backsides.
"My wife," says the first, "can't sit on a normal chair. With her ass she needs a whole bench."
"That's nothing," says the second, "My wife gets stuck in the toilet bowl at least twice a week, and I have to pull her out."
"My wife has blue eyes," says the third man.
"What's that got to do with anything?" ask his friends.
"All the rest is her backside," he answers.

"Doc, you've got to help me – I eat chicken, I shit chicken; I eat corn, I shit corn; I eat rice, I shit rice."
"You know what? Eat shit…"

A man to his psychiatrist: "Doctor, I'm in love with a horse."
"Male or female?" asks the doctor.
"I didn't say I was gay."

Carrot soup! Again?

Three whores are brought in front of a judge.
"What's your profession?" he asks the first.
"I'm a teacher," answers the whore.
"And you, what do you do for a living?" he asks the second.
"I'm also a teacher," she says.
Angry, he turns to the last one and says: "What about you?"
"I'm a whore."
"And how is business?" asks the judge.
"Not good," replies the whore, "there's too many teachers around."

Three men were jailed in an experimental facility: an American, a
Frenchman and an Irishman. They were all given one wish before they
were closed up for twenty years in total isolation. The American asked
for beer, the Frenchman asked for a woman and the Irishman asked
for cigarettes.
Twenty years later, T.V., radio and newspaper crews arrived to cover the
prisoners' stories.
They found the American drunk and singing to himself and the
Frenchman embracing his woman with five kids running around the cell.
Finally, they came to the Irishman's cell. There he was, sitting on a huge
pile of cigarettes, totally depressed, murmuring, "Anyone have a light?"

A whore is approached by a man with a strange deal: she'll get $1000 if she lets him shit on her. The whore thinks it over, and, due to her finnancial situation, finally agrees. She undresses, the man shits on her stomach, wipes, pays her the amount he promised, and leaves.
The next day, same deal: she undresses, he shits on her stomach, wipes, pays and leaves.
This continues for two weeks. The next day, the man comes over, pulls down his pants, squeezes, and nothing happens. He tries again, and again nothing happens. The whore, lying underneath him, says: "What's the matter, sweetheart, don't you love me anymore?"

American, French and Israeli couples are at a restaurant. The American turns to his wife and says, "Pass the sugar, sugar." The French husband says to his wife, "Pass the sherry, cherie." The Israeli turns to his wife and says, "Pass the steak, you cow!"

Two flies set a date at a restaurant. He gets there first and waits for her for an entire hour. Depressed, he goes back home where he sits down to watch TV.
The phone rings. She's on the line.
"Why did you stand me up?" he asks angrily.
"Oh, I'm sorry," says she, "I got stuck in a Jewish wallet."

An ant and an elephant spend a wonderful erotic night together. In the morning, as the ant wakes up, she is horrified to discover that the elephant has died.
"Oh God," wails the ant, "for one night of fun I have to dig a grave for the rest of my life!"

An exterminator comes to a farm and offers the farmer a new product. When he sees the farmer hesitate, he suggests, "I'll make a special deal with you. You tie me – naked – to a tree for the night, and rub the cream on my body. If in the morning, there's not a single bite on my body, you agree to buy ten jars of this cream. If there's as much as a hint of a bite, I will compensate you for your trouble."
In the morning, when the farmer comes to release him, he finds the agent on the verge of collapse. There's not a single bite on his body, but his dick is shriveled and bloody. The agent whispers to him, "Why didn't you tell me that your lamb doesn't have a mother?"

When a girl tells you her brother gave her a gold ring, you know that either the gold is fake or the brother is fake.

The Hunter and the Bear

A true story

A hunter marches into the forest. Suddenly, he sees a bear approaching. He aims his rifle and shoots the bear in the shoulder. The bear jumps the hunter, grabs him in both hands and asks, "Was that meant to kill me?"
"Yes," says the hunter, "it was."
"OK," says the bear, "shall I kill you or screw your ass?"
"Well, screw me," answers the hunter. The bear goes at it with vigor and lets the hunter go when he's finished. Several days later the hunter decides to settle the score with the bear and returns to the forest. This time he takes a submachine gun. As soon as he sees the bear he lets out a long burst from the gun, but only succeeds in slightly wounding the bear. As before, the bear jumps the hunter, grabs him in a Nelson and asks, "Was that meant to kill me? What'll it be, shall I kill you or screw your ass?"
"Don't kill me," pleads the hunter, "just get it over with!" So the bear screws him and then lets him go.
Several days later, the hunter tries again. This time he takes a bazooka. He climbs a tree and waits for the bear. When he's got him in sight, he lets fly. A few seconds later the bear appears out of the smoke. "Well, well, we meet again. What'll it be this time?"
"I'd rather live," admits the hunter, "so I guess you'd better get it over with."
"Tell me," says the bear, "are you a hunter or a fuckin' faggot?"

Susan has a wooden leg. One day she meets a guy and invites him upstairs. While he is in the bathroom, she undresses and puts her wooden leg on the dresser, gets into bed and turns off the light. The guy gets into bed and starts kissing and caressing her. His hands go lower and lower… "Where's your other leg?" he asks, surprised.
"On the dresser," she replies.
"Wow," says the amazed guy. "You sure are flexible!"

Coming for the
Therapist
The advice column of Dr. P. Anus

Q: My bonny lies over the ocean …
what should I do?

Miss McDublin
69 Back Rd. Englewood, Montana

Dear Miss M: Nothing. Just make sure the money goes into your Swiss bank account.

Dad, how did I come into the world?
The stork brought you, son.
And who brought you, dad?
The stork brought me too, son.
And who brought Grandpa?
The stork brought him too, son.
You mean you guys haven't fucked in three generations?

A man goes into a video rental store and asks: "Do you have the movie 'The Generous Scot'?"
"Second floor" was the prompt reply, "next to Mother Goose and Little Red Riding Hood on the fiction shelves.

What do you call the meat at the tip of a man's penis?
Woman!

Carlos is traveling by train. A violinist sits opposite him. Politely, Carlos asks him to stop playing. Says the violinist, "I'm practicing now, and when we get to New York I have a performance."
Fifteen minutes later the guy is still playing. Again, Carlos asks him to stop and the guy answers, "Practice now, performance in New York." Carlos is pissed off, pulls out his dick and starts jerking off.
"What are you doing?" asks the violinist with surprise.
Says Carlos, "I'm practicing now, and will perform on you in New York."

"Excuse me, where is 5th Avenue?" a tourist asks Franco.
"Follow me," says Franco and takes the man to the Empire State building. They go up to the observation deck and stand by the ledge.
"What do you see down there?" Franco asks.
"People," answers the man.
"How many?"
"Thousands," says the man.
"So, out of all these people you had to pick me?!"

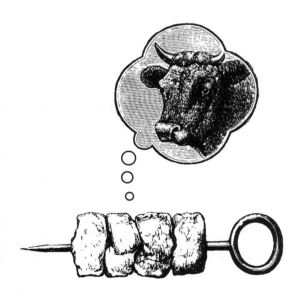

A young man gets on the bus and stands behind an old woman.
"Excuse me, young man," says the old woman, "do you want to fuck me?"
"No, way!" says he.
"Then would you mind moving over, perhaps someone else would."

A Mormon couple and their ten kids are taking a walk. Suddenly, one of the kids falls into a mud puddle.
Samuel asks his wife: "Tell me, Katherine, should we wash him or just make another one?"

A circus owner is stuck without a lion tamer a day before the show. He advertizes in the paper, and the next day two people answer the ad: a gorgeous woman and a young man. Although neither look too professional, the manager decides to let them show their stuff, saying, "This is a very dangerous lion. You have a chair, a whip and a gun at your disposal. Let's see what you can do. Ladies first."
The woman ignores the whip and the gun and walks straight into the cage. The lion sees her, perks up and is about to jump when the woman takes off her coat, and stands there stark naked. The lion crawls on its belly, purring like a pussycat, and licks her body gently.
"Bravo!" yells the manager. "Well?" he turns to the man, "Do you think you can top this?"
"Sure," says the man confidently, "just get rid of the ridiculous lion and I'll show you…"

SECOND
MOVEMENT

Joe comes home from work. As he opens the door, his wife jumps on him, pulls down his pants and starts blowing him. He gives her a look and says: "Rosie, what did you do to the car?"

How many time have I told you not to dial 1-900?

Two friends are traveling. Their car breaks down in a remote place due to an oil leak. There's no spare oil to get them to a garage, so one turns to the other and says: "If we can find some vaseline, we can go on it until we find a garage. Let's look around, maybe we can get some in one of the houses nearby."

After a while, they spot a house about a hundred yards away. In it the family is arguing over who will wash the dishes. Neither the parents nor the two daughters have volunteered for the task. The father proposes a solution – the first one to speak will wash the dishes.

By this time the two travelers have reached the house. They knock on the door but get no answer. They knock again - the same response. Having opened the door and seeing the family, they try to speak to them, again with no response, so they conclude that the family is deaf and dumb. They start to fool around with one of the daughters, and when she doesn't refuse, screw her. The same thing happens with the other daughter and the mother. They are finally going to leave when they remember why they were there in the first place, so they turn to the father and ask him for some vaseline. The father, unable to take it any longer, replies: "That does it! I'll wash the dishes."

What three words would you rather not hear when you're having sex?
"Honey, I'm home..."

An American and an Iraqi meet. The American boasts about the wonders of American democracy.
"Where I come from, I can stand in the center of Washington Square and scream 'Clinton is a bastard', at the top of my voice and no one will do anything to me."
"So what?" says the Iraqi, "I can stand in the middle of Baghdad and scream 'Clinton is a bastard' at the top of my voice, and no one will do anything to me either."

Two kids are talking.
"How old are you?"
"Six. And you?"
"Don't know."
"Don't know? Do you think about girls?"
"No."
"Well, you must be five!"

A Polack farmer had two horses, but couldn't tell them apart. He thought long and hard until he had an idea: he'd cut off one horse's tail. Now he had no problem telling one from the other.

Months went by and one day the other horse's tail was accidently cut off. Now the farmer couldn't tell his horses apart. Once again, he thought and thought until he came up with the idea of cutting off one of the horses' right ear. Now he could again tell which was which. Soon after, the other horse's right ear was also accidently cut off. Again the farmer couldn't tell them apart. That's when it hit him – one horse must be taller than the other! So he stood them side by side, and realized that the black horse was taller than the white one…

"My husband acts like a dog at home."
"You mean he does it on all fours?"
"Oh, no! He pees in the plant."

Isn't Silicon great?

... AND GOD CREATED WOMAN!

A Polack had pains in his back, so he went to the doctor. After a careful examination, the doctor gave him some suppositories and sent him home. A week later, the Polack was back. Not only did he still have pain, but it was worse. "Tell me," said the doctor, "did you take the suppositories like I told you to?"
"Of course!" replied the Pole, "Do you think I shoved them up my ass?"

A Texan's wife dies. He calls the local paper and asks to place an obituary saying, 'Sue's dead'. The operator tells him there's a six word minimum per obituary for the same price. "In that case, would you please add: 'Selling Chevy pickup 555-3867'?"

CONFIDENTIAL INFORMATION

A famous rabbi dies. At the Pearly Gates he meets the angel Gabriel. "You were a great rabbi. Your only sin was to look occasionally at women in short dresses. Therefore, you may remain in heaven but your punishment will be to have an ugly mate."
The rabbi lives his life in heaven with his ugly mate when one day he sees Sammy Davis Jr., and on his arm an absolutely stunning woman.
"Tell me, Sammy," says the rabbi, "I was a great rabbi and my only sin was looking at the occasional leg. My punishment is to spend my time in heaven with this creature, and you, who weren't virtuous, to put it mildly, got this unbelievable creation of life. Where is justice?"
"Well," says Sammy, "I'm her punishment!"

A Mexican and his wife are at the railway station. "Has the five o'clock train left yet?" asks the husband.
"Ten minutes ago," replies the conductor.
"And when is the next one?" asks the Mexican.
"In an hour."
"There are no other trains due before that?"
"No."
"What about a freight train?" continues the Mexican.
"None."
"Are you sure?"
"Of course I'm sure!" replies the now angry conductor.
"Come on," says the Mexican to his wife, "It's safe to cross the tracks now..."

A man is sitting on a train. A beautiful woman reading a book about sex is sitting opposite him. He tries to peep and find out what she's reading but can't quite see anything. At the end of the ride he approaches her, saying, "You seemed really absorbed in your book, what were you reading about?"

"It says," answers the woman, "that black men have the longest penises and Jews have the widest."

"Well, it's a pleasure to meet you! My name is Martin Luther Cohen."

Two friends are pissing in the men's room. One of them looks over at his friend's dick and sees the letters W and Y tattooed on it.

"What does that stand for?" he asks.

"It's my girlfriend's name," the friend answers. "Her name is Winny. When I get a hard on you can see the I N N.'

Some days later the guy goes to the john again and sees a black man pissing – W and Y tattooed on his dick.

"I guess your girlfriend's name is Winny," he says to the man.

"No," answers the guy, "it says 'WELCOME TO JAMAICA, ENJOY YOUR STAY'!"

Rubinstein, the man with the largest dick in Britain, died. At the funeral, an American tourist says: "I've got to buy this for my wife." "You can't!" say the relatives, "You should respect the dead." "I'll pay a million dollars," says the American. "Respect can wait," say the relatives, cut off the organ and give it to the tourist. He packs the gift in a huge suitcase and goes home to Brooklyn. As he comes in the house, he yells to his wife, "Sarah, you'll never believe what I brought for you." Sarah comes running from the kitchen, looks at the open suitcase and goes white. "Oy vey," she says, "Rubinstein's dead?"

Hey creep! Keep your wings off me

What did the blonde's mom say before she left for a date? "If you're not in bed by 10, come home!"

A woman calls her gynecologist in a flurry of worry. "Doctor, you must help me! Did I leave my panties in your office?" "Sorry, there are no panties here," says he. "Well, thank you. I'll have to try my dentist."

An Irishwoman walks down the street with only half an umbrella.
"Why only half?" asks a passerby.
"The radio said that it's going to be partly cloudy."

"You are such a shallow person! All you think and talk about is sex.
Can't you talk about anything else?"
"Like what?"
"Like politics, for instance."
"I can talk politics."
"Let's hear you."
"How many times, on the average, do you think the guys in the Senate
do it?"

It's your fault we always lose!

A horse enters a hotel accompanied by his dog.
"I'd like a room with a bathroom and a double bed," says the horse to the
desk clerk.
"Here you go," says the clerk and hands him the keys. As the horse
walks away the clerk shouts after him, "But no dogs allowed."

"Tell me," says the Polack's wife, "did you carry on long after I fell
asleep?"

"You know, I was a real idiot when I married you."
"I know, I was hoping you'd change!"

Roger comes home late one night.
"What time is it?" asks his wife from the bedroom.
"Ten", answers Roger. Just then the cuckoo clock strikes one.
"If it's ten, why did the clock strike only once?" asks the wife.
"What's your problem?" retorts Roger, "Do you expect to hear it strike the zero too?"

What did the bimbo say when she found out she was pregnant?
"I hope it's mine!"

I remember you! You were before George and after Sid at
the New Year's Eve free for all ...

T.J. was known for his foul mouth. As luck would have it, Ruthie fell in love with him. After much persuasion, Ruthie took him to her parents' house for dinner with the promise that he wouldn't use any bad language, and would impress the parents. T.J. was as good as his word and bit his tongue so he wouldn't embarrass her.

At the end of dinner, Ruthie's mother served coffee, but forgot to give T.J. a teaspoon. As the coffee turned cold Ruthie's mother asked him sweetly "Why aren't you drinking your coffee, dear? It's getting cold."

T.J. looks at her and says "What do you expect me to stir the coffee with – my dick?"

Will I really drown if you take your finger out ?

"Sam, I hear you are adopted – serves you right."

"It's true, but my parents chose me from hundreds of kids. Your parents simply didn't have a choice!"

A horny Bedouin is walking in the desert. He decides to fuck his camel. He climbs the camel, but before he can penetrate, the camel jumps forward. Every time he tries, the camel jumps forward. After many miles of trying, the Bedouin spots a beautiful woman standing by the raised hood of a car.

"I will do anything for you," says the woman, "if only you fix my car. I've been stuck here for a long time."

The Bedouin goes to work and quick as a flash fixes the car.

"And now, what can I do for you?" asks the woman.

"Would you mind holding my camel for me?"

A little kid is walking in the street, crying his eyes out. A kind woman sees him crying and asks, "Why are you crying, sweet little boy?"
"Mommy and daddy are fighting. They're throwing things at each other," answers the boy.
"Whose son are you?" asks the woman.
"That's exactly what they're fighting about."

A wife caught her husband with a young, attractive girl, and was about to throw something big and heavy at him, when he tried to explain. "She needed a ride so I gave her a ride. Then she said she was hungry, so I brought her home and fed her. Then I saw that her shoes were all worn out, so I gave her a pair of your old shoes that you haven't worn in years. Then I saw that her pants had holes in them, so I gave her a pair of your pants, ones you haven't worn since 1975. I also gave her one of your old shirts that you never wear, to replace the tattered one she was wearing. Then, as she was about to leave she asked me, "Isn't there anything else your wife doesn't use anymore?"

How do you say 'virgin' in French?
There's no such word in French.

You swing like a madman and don't look left or right. You don't keep your distance or signal like everyone else! Do you want to kill us?

"What do you call a man with a torn rubber?
-Daddy

This guy goes to the whorehouse and asks for a girl.
"How much?" asks the clerk.
"50 bucks," says he.
"First door on the right," says the clerk.
The guy follows his instructions and finds another clerk.
"How tall?" asks the second clerk.
"What's the difference?" he asks. "You know what, make her tall."
The guy is given directions again, follows them and finds himself face to face with yet another clerk who asks him what color hair he'd like his choice to have.
And so he goes from door to clerk, to door to clerk for a full two hours – eye color, fat, thin and so on. Finally, he's back at the first clerk.
"You're driving me crazy! For two hours I've been talking to clerks and opening doors," says the guy.
"Well, screwing aside," said the clerk, "was the service good?"

"What can I tell you, Bev, my ass of an husband is impossible to please. Whatever I do isn't enough. Tell me, do you find it hard to please your husband?"
"I don't know, I never tried…"

What's long, white and lies on the bottom of the ocean?
Moby's dick.

Two cannibals are eating from a big pot when one turns to the other and says, "You know, I can't stand my mother-in-law."
"Well, there's lots of rice, so you don't have to eat her…"

Arnold is in bed with his girl for the first time. After the smoke clears he asks her: "Have you had many other men?"
The girl doesn't answer.
After a few moments of silence, Arnold gently asks her, "Did I offend you? Is that why you're so quiet?"
"No," she replies, "I'm counting!"

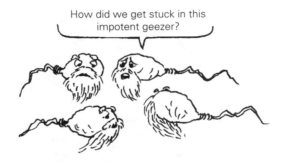

A woman was desperate. Her husband was impotent. She tried everything. She would greet him with kisses and rub up against him, but nothing happened. She wore the sexiest lingerie but her husband didn't respond. She tried love games, but his pecker was in a coma. In her despair she arranged for hypnosis therapy. After only a few appointments, her husband was up to par. They made love every night, sometimes even three times a night. There was just one thing she couldn't understand. Before they made love, her husband would go to the bathroom and return ready for action. She didn't want to ruin a good thing, but after a while curiosity got the better of her and she decided to follow him.
That night she toyed with his dick, but it didn't respond, and he, as usual, went to the bathroom. She spied on him through the keyhole. There was her husband, facing the wall, eyes closed, mumbling over and over, "It's not my wife… "

A guy gets on the bus and sits next to an extremely beautiful nun. Without thinking he puts his hand on her thigh. She turns around and sleps him hard on the cheek.

The bus driver, who had seen the whole scene through his rear view mirror, motions the guy over. "I know this nun. Go to the woods near the abbey tonight - she always prays there".

That night, the guy goes to the woods, and just as the driver had promised, the nun shows up for her nightly prayers. As soon as he sees her, the guy approachs her, telling her that God has appeared to him and that he was destined to be the father of the messiah, but only if he plants his seed that very night at that exact hour. The nun agrees to have sex with the guy - after all, it is God's will. However, she says, she's on the rag, and he'll have to enter her from behind. When they finish, the guy turns to the nun and says, "Look, I must confess, I'm not God's messenger, I just told you that because I wanted to sleep with you and I thought it would work.

Answers the nun: "I have something to confess too. I'm the bus driver."

You look about my husband's size. Would you mind trying this on?

"**Y**ou know, doctor, it's very strange," says a woman to her doctor, "whenever I sneeze continuously I have an orgasm."
"Very interesting!" says the doctor. "What have you done about it so far?"
"Well, I've been sniffing black pepper..."

Can I be on top, just this once?

Fred was on his deathbed when his best friend and partner in business, Harry, came to see him.
"Listen, Harry", says Fred in a frail whisper, "I have to confess to you. For twenty years we've been partners in business, and for twenty years I've stolen more than $100,000. I sold one of our patents to the competition, and if that isn't enough I've been sleeping with your wife."
"I want to confess something too, replies Harry, "I'm the guy who poisoned you."

A man gets on a bus with standing room only. He sees a fat woman sitting on one of the double seats in the back all by herself.
"Excuse me, would you mind moving over so I can sit down?"
"I'm very sorry," answers the woman, "I can't move because my butt fell asleep."
"That's a lame excuse," shouts the man.
"It's true," says the man sitting behind the fat woman, "I can hear it snoring from here."

What do women's breasts and toy trains have in common?
They both belong to the kid and Daddy plays with them.

Two eight year-olds are playing outside when they spot a gorgeous babe across the street.
"Let's fuck her," says one.
"Yeah, let's," says his friend, "but... who's gonna cross the street with us?"

Three husbands whose wives are learning to drive are sitting toghether one day, crying into their beers.
Says one: "Since my wife started learning to drive, it's been a nightmare trying to sleep near her. She's always pumping my balls with her foot saying: 'Brakes, clutch, brakes, clutch, brakes, clutch...'"
Says the second: "Mine grabs my dick and pulls it back and forth all night saying: 'First, second, third, reverse, first, second, third, reverse...'"
"You know, at my house, it's really a nightmare", says the third, "From the moment I get into bed my wife makes it stand, then she grabs it, pulls it to a 45 degree angle and says in that tone of voice you can't argue with, 'Fill her up.'"

A couple go out to dinner. Shortly after they sit down, an attractive young woman enters the restaurant, winks at the man and sits at a table nearby.

"Who's that?" asks the wife suspiciously.

"Believe me," sighs the husband, "it'll be tougher explaining to her who you are…"

I said between **his** legs and **only** in an emergency.

What do elephants use as a vibrator?
- A python with Parkinson.

Father and son are walking in the meadow. Suddenly the boy sees a donkey with its dick hanging out.

"Daddy, what is that?" asks the kid in amazement.

"He's got a disease," says the father.

A week later the boy and his mommy are at the zoo, and he sees a donkey with its dick hanging out.

"Mommy, look, that donkey has a disease," yells the boy.

"Disease?" sighs Mommy, "I wish your daddy had such a disease…"

Two women are talking about their kids. One says, "I don't know what to do! It takes me over an hour to put my baby to sleep every night."
"Not me," replies her friend, "when I want my baby to sleep I simply throw him in the air a couple of times."
Surprised, her friend asks, "How does it work?"
"It's very simple," she replies, "the ceiling is very low."

A woman knocks on her neighbor's door and asks if she may borrow her dishwasher.
"Sure," says her friend. "Joe, the neighbor wants you!"

What's the difference between a bar and a clitoris?
Most men can find the bar.

This is the third time you've had to pee in the last hour!

Poodle and Doberman meet at the vet's. "Why are you here?" asks the poodle.

"Well," says the doberman, "a few days ago I was really horny so I fucked the pillow, then the mattress, and then I ran outside and fucked every bitch in sight. I'm here to be neutered. What about you?"

"I also got horny a few days ago," says the poodle, "so I fucked the pillow, then the mattress and then I ran into the kitchen, saw my master's wife washing the dishes so I fucked her from behind."

"So I guess they're going to neuter you too?"

"No, I'm here for a manicure."

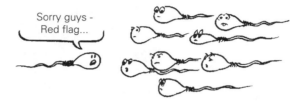

A man checks into a hotel and goes to his room. About an hour later he comes back down to the desk and demands to see the manager.

"Yes, sir, how may I help you?" asks the manager.

"What kind of hotel is this?" shouts the man, "I get in my room and there's a shotgun barrel staring at me. Before I can say anything, the man behind the gun tells me to get down on my knees and blow him, and if I don't, he'll blow me away."

"So what did you do?" enquires the manager.

"What did I do? What do you think I did? You didn't hear any gunshots, did you?"

... AND DILDO DONNA SAYS:
When a man tells you he's a sex machine,
check his plug!

This guy is about to go on a cruise. "Listen," says his pal, "I once went on a cruise. It's wild. The babes are hot, and it's a party! You should buy at least one hundred condoms, and since you might get seasick, get some anti-nausea pills." With this information in hand, our man goes to the drugstore.

The pharmacist, happy to make the sale, cannot contain his curiousity. Says he, "Pardon my asking, but if you get so sick from it, why do you do it so often?"

On her honeymoon a young Italian bride runs from the bedroom to her mother in the kitchen, crying, "Mama, he's got a hairy chest!"
"Never mind," says her mother, "many men have. Go back to him. Meanwhile, I will make ravioli."
A few minutes later, the bride again comes running into the kitchen and says, "Mama, he's got scars on his stomach!"
"Never mind," says Mama, "many men have. Go back to him, and I'll make ravioli."
The bride goes back to her groom and sees that he's missing half a foot. She runs to the kitchen, screaming: "Mama, he pulled down his pants and… and… he's only got half a foot."
"You know what?" says Mama, "YOU make the ravioli and I'll go to him!"

Joe has an awful headache. He goes to the doctor.
"The best thing for headaches is a teaspoon of coffee taken rectally,"
says the doctor.
"But Doc…"
"It's the only proven cure," says the doctor.
Joe continues to suffer. One day, he can't take it anymore. He goes back
to the doctor, bends over and lets him shove a teaspoon of coffee up
his ass.
"Arghhhhh…" whimpers Joe.
"What's wrong?" asks the doctor. "Did it hurt?"
"No," says Joe, "you forgot the sugar."

**That's it! That's the last one. Now we'll have peace
and quiet for a few million years.**

A guy goes to a whorehouse with three bucks in his pocket.
"We don't have a whore for three bucks," says the madam, "but for this
amount you can fuck a goat."
The guy, who was really horny, agreed and fucked the goat.
Two weeks later he comes back to the whorehouse with one dollar in his
pocket.
"For a buck I can't even give you the goat, but it's enough for the peep
show." says the madam.
The guy pays his buck and goes in. There, through a one-way window,
he joins a lot of other people watching a man masturbating a donkey.
"I've never seen anyone rubbing a donkey before," says the guy to a man
standing next to him.
"This is nothing," says the man, "you should have been here two weeks
ago – some guy fucked a goat!"

Why do women prefer older gynecologists?
Because their fingers shake.

A man phones home and asks the butler for his wife.
"I can't right now," says the butler, "she's busy."
"Doing what?" inquires the husband.
"She's in the bedroom."
"Is she alone?"
"No," answers the butler, "she's with a man."
"Listen carefully," instructs the husband, "there's a gun in the drawer under the phone, take it out."
"Yes, sir."
"Good. Now go to the bedroom and shoot both of them."
The butler puts the phone down and the husband hears footsteps, two shots and footsteps again.
"Did you kill them?" he asks.
"Yes, sir."
"Very good. Now open the window above you and throw the gun in the pool so that it won't be found."
"Into the pool, sir?" asks the butler in surprise. "But we don't have a pool!"
"Is this 555-5432…?"

A gigolo, known for his success with the opposite sex, married a woman with a limp.
"Now, seriously, Don Juan," said his friends, "should such a successful gigolo marry someone like her?"
"You just don't understand," says Donny, "She's just terrific. When I undress her, I stand, naked, behind her. Then I put a beer can under her shorter foot and penetrate her from behind. When I'm in, I kick away the can, and when she starts looking for it with her leg…"

In the year 2024 the ozone disintegrated and a great fire spread throughout the world. The only survivors were two monkeys who hid far back in a cave. When all was quiet they emerged and looked around gravely.
One turned to his mate and said, "Well, darling, I guess we'll have to start all over again!"

Coming for the
Therapist
The advice column of Dr. P. Anus

Q: How many times should I close my eyes and count to 10 before something happens?

Virginia Virgin

A: Instead of counting numbers, try doing them – you'll be surprised at the results.
PS: In cases such as yours I make house calls.

A man was hospitalized in the psycho ward because he thought he was a mouse. After long tender treatment, he was released. He left the institute but soon came running back, pale and horrified.
"What's the matter?" asked the doctor.
"There's a cat outside."
"But you're healthy now, you are no longer a mouse." said the doctor soothingly.
"Yeah," answered the man, "suppose the cat doesn't know that yet?"

THIRD
MOVEMENT

What does a man do after beating his wife in an argument?
Apologize.

A man sends his wife out to buy an electric saw.
"I'm sorry, ma'am, we're out of electric saws," says the salesman, "But I have a great new item that should do the trick - a trained parrot."
"A parrot? I don't under..."
"Watch," says the salesman. "this is a very special parrot."
"Parrot," commands the salesman, "the table!"
Immediately, the parrot jumps on to the table, and in a matter of seconds saws it in half.
"Parrot," commands the salesman, "the chair!" Within seconds, the chair is in little pieces.
The wife, duly impressed, buyst the parrot and takes him home. When her husband comes home from work that night, he asks about the saw. With a smile, his wife tells him: "They didn't have an electric saw, but they had this parrot."
"What the hell are you talking about!" shouts the man. "I wanted an electric saw and you bought a parrot! Parrot my ass..."

Well if you ask me, their behavior patterns indicate that they are Honeysuckles

I tell you, my wife's an angel.
You're lucky, mine is still alive.

Boss to secretary: "What did my wife say when you told her I'd be two hours late?"
Secretary: "She asked if she could count on it."

A man is on a business trip in Chicago, and since he's far from home he arranges for a call girl to pass the time with him. In the morning she names her price. The man is suprised at how low it is. He says "You know, your services are easily worth more money."
"Don't worry," says the call girl, "this payment is pocket money. The big money comes from blackmail!"

Yo Mr Patrolman

I'm leaving my car under your ~~watchful~~ evil eye and in your good care while I do this deal with the boys. I'll only be a few minutes, but if I feel like it, I'll stay longer, so I'm warning you, don't give me a ticket, cause I'll get your Mama, and fuck her up big time, and I won't forget your wife either, so don't say I didn't warn you, and remember I know your address.

No Thanks necessary

Bruno
(you know which one)

A young couple gets married. After the honeymoon the woman says to her husband:
"Well, it's time to go to work."
"No need," says the husband.
"What will we live on, then?"
"We'll live on love, love, love," says he.
A week later, the same scene and the same answer: "We'll live on love."
Two weeks go by. The wife is starving, but she keeps getting the same reply from her husband. He goes out for a walk. When he returns, an hour later, he sees his wife going up the stairs and sliding down the banister, over and over again.
"What on earth are you doing?" says he.
"Warming lunch!"

An elderly couple are celebrating their 50th anniversary with a touch of romance. They prepare a festive meal, light some candles and sit at the table naked.
"Oh, Mendel," says the woman, "how wonderful this is, my heart is filled with warmth."
"Well, it's a small wonder," says her husband, "your breast is in the soup..."

Two kids are arguing. One says, "My daddy's better than your daddy!" "Oh, yeah? My mommy's better than your mommy," counters the other. "That's true," says the first, "even my daddy says so!"

A farmer is on his way to market to sell his produce. He puts his wife in the back of the pickup so she can watch the produce. The road is very bumpy and the pickup bounces up and down. A few minutes into the ride the wife bangs on the roof of the truck and yells to her husband to stop. When he does, she says, "I'm really horny. Let's go into the bushes and do it."
They do it, get back in the pickup and continue to drive. Fifteen minutes later, the wife bangs on the roof and asks her husband to stop. Again they hit the bushes. After the third time, he says to her: "Do me a favor, I have to get to market on time. Would you get off the cucumbers and sit on the tomatoes…!"

A sailor passes a whorehouse. As he goes by, one of the girls propositions him, promising him something he's never had before. "I believe you," says the sailor, "that's what you told my friend last month and he's still scratching!"

A Brit, a Frog and a Polak are sentenced to death by firing squad. The Brit goes first. Just before they squeeze the trigger he yells: "Flood! Flood!" Everyone runs and he is saved.
When it's the Frenchman's turn, gun barrels pointing at him, he screams: "Earthquake! Earthquake!" and everyone runs again.
When the Pole goes before the firing squad, he yells: "Fire!"

A couple is in an elevator. On the third floor a man gets on and farts noisily.
"You should be ashamed of yourself, farting before my wife," says the angry husband.
"Oh, I'm terribly sorry, I didn't know it was her turn next."

Two Americans on a trip to Germany stop at a fast food joint. They order two glasses of milk from the buxom waitress. To their astonishment, the waitress pops out her breast and squeezes milk into two glasses. Once they recover, one says to the other, "It's good we didn't order beer..."

A man goes to the doctor.
"Help me, doc," he says, "there's a knife in my stomach."
"Are you in pain?" asks the doctor.
"Only when I laugh…"

What's the difference between a blonde and an airplane?
The black box ALWAYS tells the truth.

A horny young man goes to a whorehouse to relieve his aching balls. He approaches one of the whores and asks the traditional question, "How much?"
"FIfty bucks" comes the reply. "But I've only got thirty," begs he.
"Sorry," says the whore, "fifty it is."
He goes from room to room, asking the same question of each whore he meets and receiving the same reply of fifty. Finally, he opens the last door where he finds a black whore who gives him what he wants for thirty.
One day, his son asks him for twenty dollars. "Son, if I had twenty bucks, you'd have been white… "

Coming for the
Therapist
The advice column of Dr. P. Anus

Q: My boyfriend first snoozes, then comes. Is this natural?

Mary Lord
45 Twilight Zone Av. Pa.

A: No it's not natural, but is every thing around us natural? Are Shers tits natural? No! Is Michel Jecksons nose natural? No! Is O.J Simpson a murderer? No!

BATHROOM WORKOUTS

Have you ever sat on the toilet, humming away peacefully, and suddenly, it's gone – the most important part of your life has disappeared under those middle-age tires! No longer can you watch the action live! It wasn't always this way – once your stomach was flat, the flagpole tall... Well, we all get older, we change, work hard, and even a good sit on the old toilet has become a luxury you can't afford.

At least you can make the best of those few minutes. Following are exercises you can do in the loo which have been specially designed by the Anti-Competitive Sports Counsel of Atlanta. Happy exercising!

A. Arm workout

Sit on the toilet and raise your arms straight out to the sides (90° – not temperature, degrees of angle!) and then to the side. If your hands or arms hit the wall, it must be too close. In this case, use an up and down motion with arms in front (see drawing) until it's time to wipe. Happy wiping!

B. Forward bends

Sit up straight on the seat, back against the cover (on the assumption that you've lifted it), look straight ahead and bend forwards, keeping your back straight (see drawing). Repeat indefinitely. Note: This exercise is not intended for bathrooms in which the sink is less than 13 inches from the bowl.

C. Leg lifts

This is intended to strengthen the back muscles and improve your ability to see your toes. Sitting comfortably on the seat (and not in the bowl, as some people do), let your arms hang loosely at your sides. Bring your legs straight out in front of you (this doesn't appear in the drawing because our model was too tired to do it) and then lift your heels from the floor, which will, in theory at least, lift your legs from the floor too. Hold for a few seconds, then let go. The law of gravity states that your heels will re-encounter the floor. This should be done as many times as possible (at least twice).

D. Gravity presses

This exercise has been specially designed by our experts for constipation relief. Sitting comfortably on the seat, let your hands hang down away from the sides of the bowl, then bring them back and grab the lower part of the seat (as shown). Holding firmly, pull your body down as if you were trying to push yourself into the bowl (but make sure you don't actually succeed). Hold for several seconds, then relax. Repeat until you feel relief. This exercise is not recommended for those with weak stomachs.

An international research project on the subject of "The shape of the human penis" elicited the following results from France. "The penis is shaped so as to provide women with the utmost pleasure."
The Americans concluded that "the penis is shaped to give a man pleasure."
The Israelis sent their conclusion in last. "We have proved, beyond the shadow of a doubt, that the penis is shaped in order to prevent the owner's hand from slipping off!"

How can you tell if a woman is Puerto Rican?
She screams at you, answers for you and then tells you to stop talking nonsense.

"Dad, what does 'automatically' mean?"
"It's very simple, son, if your mother is a bitch, then automatically you become a son of a bitch."

An African tribal chief calls Tarzan one day. "Listen, bud, my wife just gave birth to a white baby. Since you're the only white man around, it must be yours. I think your day will be over in the cooking pot."
Tarzan takes the chief aside and points at the hillside: "Do you see those white sheep?"
"Yes," answers the chief.
"How do you explain the black sheep in the herd?"
"OK," says the chief. "I won't tell if you won't."

Why did you tell your friends you married me because I'm a good cook when you know I can't even boil an egg?
I needed an excuse…

An Iraqi couple were visiting the London Zoo when they came upon the skunk exhibit. The husband was immediately taken with the black and white striped creatures, snuck into the cage and took one. He hid it under his coat for the rest of their visit, but as they approached the exit he suddenly became anxious.
"Here, take it" he said, passing the skunk to his wife, "and hide it under your skirt until we get outside."
"But what about the smell?" protested his wife .
"Don't worry," said the husband, "If he dies I'll go back and steal another one."

"Listen, I hate to be the one to tell you, but your wife is cheating on you with your friend Dick"
"Dick? I barely know him."

BONER: "A babe who tells you to stop – actually means stop talking…"

Ms Zebra goes for a stroll around the animal farm. She meets the dog. "Say, Mr. Dog, what do you do here?"
"I'm the farm's watchdog," the dog replies.
She meets a hen. "What do you do here?"
"I lay eggs," says the hen proudly, "my feathers are used for pillows and they grill my husband."
"And what do you do?" she asks the sheep.
"I give milk and wool."
Finally, she meets the bull. "And you, Mr. Bull, what do you do?"
"Just take off your pajamas and I'll show you!"

Why is an expectant father like a dog? During the first three months he does it on all fours, for the next three months he licks and the last three months he sits by a hole and howls.

A bear and a rabbit are taking a crap in the forest. "Tell me," asks the bear, "Does shit stick to your fur sometimes?"
"Why no," replies the rabbit.
"Wonderful!" smiles the bear, wiping his ass with the rabbit.

What are four Americans in a Chevy van?
- "The A team".
And what are four gays in a Chevy van?
- "The Aids Team".

A police officer got off work early one day and went home. He entered the house quietly without turning the lights on, so he wouldn't wake his wife. As he undresses, hears his wife say, "Darling, I have the worst headache, please get me some aspirin at the corner store."
He dresses and leaves.
"Hey, I thought you were a cop," remarks the cashier at the corner store.
"And that I am," says the cop.
"Then why are you wearing a fireman's uniform?"

A guy goes to the doctor. "Doc," he says, "I've got cranial diarrhea."
"Cranial diarrhea? I've never heard of that."
"Yeah, I've got a lot of ideas but they're all shit."

The lion prowls the forest, his chest puffed up with pride and self admiration. Suddenly a deer crosses his path.

"Tell me," roars the lion at the deer, "who's king around here?"

"You are, of course you are," says the deer and darts quickly away. The lion continues to prowl, and comes across a fox.

"Mr. Fox," roars the lion, "who's king around here?"

"It's obvious that you, and only you are king," replies the fox, and disappears. The lion continues to prowl, drenched in self admiration and pride, when he sees an elephant enjoying his lunch. The lion approaches the elephant, roars as loud as he can, and says: "Tell me, elephant, who's king around…" but before the lion can complete his question the elephant kicks him head over heels.

"What's wrong with you?" whimpers the lion, "can't an animal ask a simple question around here?"

The convict and the hangman walk to the gallows on the day the execution is to take place.

"Jeez, it's cold, and it's pouring, too!" cries the convict.

"What are you complaining about," replies the hangman, "I have to walk back!"

A leaking cruiser,
A leaking life raft,
A leaking rubber,
What's next?

A National Geographic reporter is seeking Tarzan in the depths of the jungle. Once she finds him, she asks him about his life in the jungle and his isolation from humans. Finally, she asks, "What do you do for sex? Is there a girl to help you in that department?"

"No," said Tarzan.

"Then how do you cope with sexual desires and needs?" asks the reporter.

"Simple," says Tarzan. "Do you see that tree there? There's a hole there. When I'm horny I stick my piece in the hole and that's that."

"Would you like to try it with a real woman?" asks the reporter.

"Why not?" said Tarzan.

With no hesitation the reporter undresses. Tarzan approaches her, turns her around and kicks her in the butt.

With some pain the reporter asks curiously: "Why did you do that?"

"You see," answers Tarzan, "before I penetrate I want to make sure there aren't any squirrels around."

Mommy, where do children come from?
The stork brings them, dear.
Yeah, but who fucks the stork?

What's the best substitute for a vibrator?
A guy with Parkinson's.

An optimist is a man who gets married at 80 and looks for an apartment near a school.

Undercover dick

A couple already had three kids, But the wife wanted another baby. Her husband objected, saying, "It says in the newspaper that every fourth child born is Chinese."

A Frenchman kissed his wife good night and broke his glasses when she closed her legs.

An Iraqi was held for questioning by the CIA.
"How's the regime?" asks the investigator.
"I read in 'El-Akhbar' that it's not doing too well," answers the Iraqi.
"And the economic situation?"
"I heard on Monte Carlo radio that economically the country isn't doing too well."
"What's the standard of living like?" continues the investigator.
"On Middle East TV they mentioned that the standard of living isn't very good," says the Iraqi.
"Tell me," says the investigator finally, "why do you keep telling me what was said in the paper, on the radio and TV? Don't you have an opinion?"
"I do," answers the Iraqi, "but I don't agree with it."

How does a blonde turn on the light in the morning?
Opens the car door.

A man is invited for dinner at his friends' house. The wife serves the food and they all begin to eat. Suddenly the husband finds a hair in the potatoes and screams at his wife, "Can't you be more careful when you cook?" He takes the bowl of potatoes and throws it out the window. The wife takes the salad bowl, throws it out the window and screams, "if you don't like it, don't eat it!" At which point the husband takes the casserole and throws it out the window. Not to be outdone, the wife throws the soup tureen out after the casserole. The friend, feeling a little left out, picks up the table and throws it out the window.
"Why don't you butt out?" yells the husband.
"Oh," said the friend, "I thought we were eating out…"

When I said 30 - I meant dollars - not tricks!!!

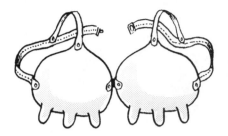

Cowgirl

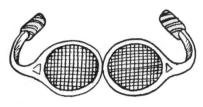

Tennis buff

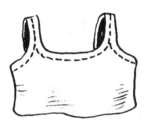

Breastless

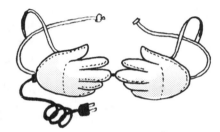

Nympho's choice

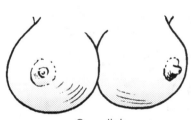

Swedish

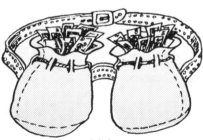

Irish

Sports commentator

Russian

Two old friends meet. Says one to the other, "My daughter has a house in Malibu, two apartments - one in New York and one in L.A. – and a neat sports car."
"Yeah, I know," says the friend, "my daughter is a call girl too."

A Mexican is sitting in the movie theater with one leg on the seat in front of him, the other on two seats next to him, his head back and his arms on either side.
"Just great," says the usher, "I bet you'd like a beer, too."
"Zip it," groans the Mexican, "Call an ambulance, quick! I just fell from the balcony!"

A Russian cosmonaut returns to earth after a visit to the moon. A local TV crew awaits him.
"So," asks the reporter, "what's it like up there?"
"There's no life up there, either."

An Englishman, an Italian and an Israeli pay their friend a visit on his birthday. The Englishman gives him a sweater that says 'made in England' on the tag. The Italian gives him a pair of shoes marked 'made in Italy' on the sole. The Israeli gives him a towel that has 'Ritz Hotel' embroidered along the edge.

Two women meet.
"I don't know what to do. Ever since I got married Bill and I aren't communicating."
"What will you do, divorce him?"
"No way! My husband's name is Mike."

A man took a gorgeous woman on a date at a restaurant. He was appalled when she ordered large quantities of the most expensive dishes on the menu. After a while he could contain himself no longer. "Do you usually eat this much at home?" he asked, "No!" came her reply, "but no one at home wants to fuck me..."

A rich old virgin wanted to marry. Only another virgin would do, so she hired a P.I. to look for such a man. The P.I. found her match in Australia. On the wedding night, after a nice long bath, the newlywed virgin enters the bedroom to find that everything except the carpet has been removed by her new husband.
"What did you do that for?" she asked.
"Well," he said, "I've never had sex with a woman before, but if it's anything like fucking a kangaroo, we'll need lots of space..."

A couple got married and had baby a year later. Three years later, they separate. During the time they spend apart, love conquers all and they decide to live together again.
After a while she asks him to marry her again.
"Are you crazy enough to think," shouts the man, "that I'd marry a divorcee with a kid?"

Little Red Riding Hood goes to visit her granny who lives in the forest. When she gets to granny's house she finds her in bed with a peculiar expression on her face.
"Granny dear," says Red, "why are your ears so big?"
"So I can hear you better," says granny.
"And why are your eyes so big?"
"So I can see you better."
"And granny," continues Red, "why is your mouth so big?"
"Well," moans granny, "did you see the hunter's tool …?"

A man comes home and finds his wife in bed with a stranger.
"How can you do this to me?" cries the husband, "you vowed to love me and me alone!"
"I told you he's stupid," turned the wife to the stranger, "What does love have to do with sex?"

The Pill is like aspirin.

If you don't forget to take the Pill, you save yourself a lot of headaches.

ONE ON ONE

My wife hasn't spoken to me for two weeks!
And how do you feel?
Far be it from me to stop her...

A bear, a lion and a rabbit are walking in the forest when suddenly it starts to pour. The three of them run to hide in a cave. A day goes by but the rain doesn't let up. Two days go by, and it's still raining cats and dogs. After five days in the cave, it's still raining. The lion says, "I'm very hungry and it doesn't look like the rain is going to stop. There's no choice – one of us has to be eaten."
The rabbit jumps between the lion and the bear and says, "I'll kill anyone who touches the bear!"

What do tofu and a vibrator have in common?
They're both meat substitutes.

FORTH
MOVEMENT

What do a doctor and a whore have in common?
They both get extra for house calls.

A man had three boys, all of whom had pitch black hair. A forth son was born, but he was blond! He kept his suspicions to himself for many years, but one day could contain himself no longer. "You know," said he to his wife, "I have a feeling that the little one isn't mine."
"Are you kidding?" replied his wife, "he's the only one that is yours!"

A guy walks down the street and meets a friend. "Hey, you'll never guess what happened to me today," says the friend. "I went to the track to check out some races. I put down a few bucks with the bookies and went to say hello to a pal. As I walk along, I noticed that my shoelace was untied. I bent over to tie it, and before I knew what was happening somebody threw a saddle on my back..."
"So, what did you do?" asks the guy.
"Do you think I had much choice?" answered the friend, "I came in second!"

An elderly lady at the movies to the man sitting in front of her: "Can't you fool around with your girlfriend somewhere else, like at home?" "Home's not such a good idea," replied he, "because at the moment my wife is there."

A Puerto Rican woman to her husband: "You were really screaming awfully loudly in your sleep."
"Who was sleeping?"

A producer goes to see a peep show that promises an amazing act – an Italian fucking 50 women, one after another. After the show, he approaches the man. "Listen, we can make a good buck out of your act. If we put on a show where you fuck 50 women, everyone will come." The Italian agrees and they sign a contract. At show time, the club is packed. The Italian goes on stage and starts his act. One... two... ten... twenty... thirty... forty... forty-five... forty-six... forty-seven... and hits the floor, unconscious. When he comes to, the producer is furious. "What have you done! You said 50 and only fucked 47, what will we do now, the crowd wants to lynch me!"
"I don't know what happened," says the Italian, "I did a full dress rehearsal this afternoon and everything was fine..."

If you don't stop contradicting me all the time, I'm gonna screw you right here, right now.
No way.

Two cannibals go to a movie with a white man.
"May I see your tickets, please," says the usher.
They show him two tickets.
"What about him?" asks the usher, pointing to the white man.
"Is there a law against bringing in candy?"

What do Saddam Hussein and his father have in common?
Neither pulled out in time.

A guy visits his friend in the country and strolls around, enjoying the fresh air. After a while he has to piss. He pulls out his dick and relieves himself. Suddenly, a snake slithers out of the bushes and bites his penis. He screams and his friend comes running. One look at his friend's swollen penis and he runs back to the house and calls the doctor. "Listen," says the doctor, "action has to be taken immediately. There's only one way to save your friend's life. Make a small x-shaped cut where the snake bit your friend and then suck out the venom. It's likely you'll save his life this way. If you don't, he'll probably die."
The guy runs back to his friend.
"So, what did the doctor say?" asks the friend, writhing in agony.
"Well," said the friend, "he said you're going to die..."

A woman was having a lot of trouble with her closet. Whenever a bus went by, the doors flew open. She called the carpenter and asked him to come over to check out the problem. The closet looked fine from the outside, so the carpenter climbed inside to see exactly what the problem was.

Just as he got into the cabinet, the woman's insanely jealous, extremely large husband came home.

Opening the clolset, he was quite surprised to find the carpenter. "What are you doing here!" shouts the angry husband.

"If I told you I were waiting for bus, would you believe me?"

A man to his wife: "I'm sick of your yelling and screaming. Everything you say to me goes in one ear and out the other."

"That's because there's nothing in between!" answers she.

A man is walking by a lake when he notices another man in the water waving his arms and yelling, "Help me, help me, I can' t swim!"
"So why are you yelling?" asks the man, "I can't swim either but I'm not making a big deal out of it, am I?"

As far as I'm concerned, our relationship is over.

Joseph died. His widowed wife consulted a channeller so that she could communicate with him. "Can you do this for me?" she asked the channeller. "Of course," the channeller replied, "but I'll need something of your husband's, like a shirt or a ring."
The wife gave the channeller her husband's ring. The channeller mumbled some magic words and within a few minutes a sound was heard.
"Joe, is that you?" asked the wife with tears in her eyes.
"Yes, it is I," answered the spirit.
"How are you?" asked the wife.
"Wonderful," came the voice of the spirit.
"Oh, Joe, what's it like over there?"
"What can I say, Sarah," answered the dead husband, "I make love and eat lettuce all day, make love and eat lettuce."
"Oh really?" asked the wife in awe, "is this what heaven is about?"
"Heaven? Who said anything about heaven?" asked the spirit. "I'm a rabbit in Australia."

What's the difference between a whore and a bowling ball?
You can only stick three fingers in a bowling ball.

...AND DILDO DONNA SAYS:
What I like about sex is – even when it's bad,
it's good!

Why don't bimbos like pickles?
They keep getting their head stuck in the
jar...

A farmer meets his friend at the general
store and starts to complain about the
new cow he's just bought. "I rented a
bull for her, but as soon as he's ready to
enter her, she moves to the right. He
tries again, this time from the right, and
she moves left. The bull keeps trying,
but she's had enough, and sits down. I
can't believe it!"
"Tell me, Joe," says his friend,
"did you buy her in Podunk?"
"Why yes," replies Joe, "how
did you know?"
"My wife is from Podunk."

When is a beaver happiest?
When it's eaten.

Two whores are walking down Sunset
Boulevard on their day off. Suddenly one
says to her friend. "Do you smell sperm?"
"Get serious," answers the other,
"I burped!"

What do you call a bimbo who dyes her
hair black?
Artificial intelligence.

During the Los Angeles riots, a police car drives through the streets of the city, "Ten minutes to curfew! Anyone not in their home by that time will be shot. I repeat, ten minutes to curfew… "

Suddenly, one of the cops pulls his gun and shoots an old man crossing the road.

"What did you do that for?" asks his astonished partner, "we just said ten minutes to curfew!"

"That's right," comes the reply, "and I know where that old man lives. He'd never have made it home in ten minutes."

A woman tells her husband, "I'm going riding, I'll be back in a couple of hours."

"Yes, I know," says the husband, "the horse called twice."

A young woman is walking home when suddenly she finds herself at the gates of the cemetery. As her fear mounts she notices a man standing next to her.

"Wow, I feel much better now," says the woman, "this place really gives me the creeps! Would you mind helping me across the cemetery where it's better lit?"

"No problem," says the man, and they start to walk across the cemetery. About halfway through, the woman asks, "Don't you find it creepy crossing the cemetery? I'm scared shitless…"

"What can I say," answered the man, "I used to be scared, when I was alive…"

A baby boy was born to a young couple and brought joy to their lives. At one year the baby hadn't uttered a word. A few months later he was still silent. At the age of three, the parents consulted a specialist and the child was diagnosed as deaf and dumb. At the age of five, during dinner, the boy suddenly says, "This food isn"t salty enough!"
"Good Lord," yells the mother, "you can speak! You're not mute?"
"Yes, I can" says the boy.
"So why haven't you spoken until now?" asks the mother
"Because up to today, everything was OK!"

You know, my wife is like a painting.
Is she so beautiful?
No, but I've been meaning to hang her for years.

Don't you think it's time the baby called me Daddy?
Don't you think we should let him mature a little before we tell him the truth?

Four cops were killed in Cuba in a car crash. Two died right away – the other two died while dramatizing the story for TV.

A man goes to the pet shop. There he sees a parrot in his cage, suspended from a pole by his dick. He decides to buy the parrot as a gift for his wife. After a few days in his new home the parrot begins to talk, "Hello! How's is going?" etc.

One day the guy comes home and the parrot says to him, "Listen – today your wife had a visitor."

"Really," says the husband, "and what were they doing?"

"They undressed and went to bed," replied the parrot.

"You don't say!" exclaims the husband. "What did they do next? Did he fuck her?"

"I don't know," said the parrot, "as soon as she undressed I got a hard on and fell off the pole!"

A young woman gets on a bus with standing room only. As the bus lurches forward she looks down with contempt at the young man sitting near her. She turns to him and snaps, "You should be ashamed of yourself – not giving up your seat for a pregnant woman."
"Are you pregnant?" he asks, "you don't look it."
"Well, what do you expect? Should it show after half an hour?"

An elderly couple are watching a religious show on TV one evening. "And now," says the preacher on the screen, "place one hand on the TV and the other on the part of your body that you want healed and I will heal it."
The woman places one hand on her leg an the other on the TV. The husband gets up from his chair, places one hand on the screen and the other on his limp dick.
"What are you doing?" asks his wife, "he specifically said he heals the sick, not raises the dead!"

Coming for the
Therapist
The advice column of Dr. P. Anus

Q: Recently my stomach is getting bigger and I get nauseated and sick. Could it be because I eat too much?

Sue C.
El Fato, Cal.

A: Yes. But for a second opinion please consult your doctor, after all, this is a sex therapy column, not a diet column.

What's the difference between a Cuban and a film?
A film can be developed.

On a Delta Airlines flight to Hawaii, the captain makes the following announcement:
"Good afternoon, ladies and gentlemen. Due to a technical problem in the engines I have to make an emergency landing at sea. Those of you who can swim, please take a seat on the right side of the plane. Those of you who can't swim, please take a seat on the left side. As soon as the plane touches the water, the emergency slides will inflate. Those on the right side of the plane should approach the doors and slide down the slides. Once you reach the water, there will be a 300 yard swim until you reach the lifeboats.
Those of you sitting on the left side of the plane, thank you for flying Delta..."

A fireman had a bad accident – he slipped on a pipe and needed an operation. "Look," says the surgeon as the fireman lies on the operating table, "one of your balls is gone, but I'm going to try something new. I'll replace it with an onion." Due to his condition the fireman had little choice but to agree. Two weeks later, he comes in to see the surgeon for a checkup. "Well, how's your sex life with your new ball?" asks the surgeon. "Well, doc, I'll tell you," replies the fireman, "everything's just great, but when my girlfriend blows me, she always starts to cry..."

A Jewish man relates the following: "When I was born, my mother looked at my nose, and said to my dad: 'Joseph, call the doctor, quick! They've made a terrible mistake – they took the baby and left the stork!'"

A guy is visiting his Polish friend on his farm. As he's being shown around, he sees a sheep's ass pointing straight at him. "Wow!" says he, "I wish that were Cindy Crawford!"
"Cindy shmindy," replies his friend, "I wish it were dark!"

A woman goes to her gynecologist and undresses at his request. She lies down – the doctor begins to fondle her breasts, especially her nipples.

"Do you know what I'm doing?" asks the doctor.

"Yes," answered the woman, "you are checking my breasts for breast cancer."

Next, the doctor puts his hand between her legs and explores her vagina with his finger. "Do you know what I'm doing now?" he asks.

"Of course," she says, "you're checking if I have any kind of vaginal infection."

The doctor then pulls down his pants and penetrates the woman.

"And do you know what I'm doing now?"

"Sure," says the woman, "you're getting AIDS."

A Polish pilot goes out on his maiden flight. Finally, with great difficulty, he manages to land the plane. "Wow," says the pilot to his instructor, "that was really hard. Do you know how short the strip is?"

"Sure," replies the instructor, "but did you notice how wide it is?"

A man goes to the doctor.
"Help me, doc," he says, "there's a knife in my stomach."
"Are you in pain?" asks the doctor.
"Only when I laugh…"

An American and a Polack were sentenced to death. They told the American he could choose between hanging, an injection or the electric chair. The American thought about it for a minute and said: "An injection hurts, hanging chokes… give me the electric chair."
They strapped him into the chair, threw the switch, and… nothing happened, so they set him free.
They asked the Polack what he preferred. Hesitating only slightly, he replied, "Hanging chokes. I hear the electric chair doesn't work… so give me an injection."

What does a bimbo say after making love?
"Thanks, guys…"

Why isn't a bimbo like the Titanic?
We know how many men went down on the Titanic.

One fine winter's day, Bill Clinton looks out his window and discovers that someone has written "Fuck you Bill!" in urine in the freshly fallen snow. He immediately calls the head of White House security and orders him to find the perpetrator. Several hours later, the head of security is waiting for him as he comes out of a meeting. "Sir," says he, "we have found the perpetrator. The urine is Al Gore's."
"What!" exclaims Clinton, "How can he do this to me! Bring him to me at once!"
"Sir, with all due respect, I don't think that's a very good idea," interjects the security chief, "the handwriting is your wife's."

Why did 18 bimbos go to the R-rated movie?
Because they heard that under 17 would not be admitted.

What do four bimbos have in common?
Nothing they can think of.

Why are girls who sound so nice on the phone so ugly when you meet them?

BE A TELEPATH

Let say you've spotted a juicy prospect and started up a conversation. Here's a quick and easy way to impress her and get her birthday (this may be accomplished sitting down, too). Just ask her to:

1. Multiply the day (1-31) of her birth by three.
2. Now add five.
3. Multiply by four.
4. Add the day and month.
5. Subtract 20.
Then ask her to tell you the number she's gotten.

When she does, divide the result by thirteen. You will then get the day and the remainder is the month. For example: The result was 253. Divide by thirteen and you get 19, remainder 6. The person was born on the nineteenth of June.

Editor's note: Make sure both you and the obfect did the math correctly. One small mistake and your/our reputation goes up in smoke.

It's that damn Tsetse fly! There goes the neighborhood.

Two gay guys meet in the street.
"How's it going" asks one.
"Great! There's no time to fart."

There's no place like home!

A kid had a Jewish mother and a Puerto Rican father. One day the kid comes home and asks his mother, "Am I more Jewish or more Puerto Rican?"
"Why do you ask, bubbeleh?" replies his mother.
"Well, there's this kid who wants to sell me his bike," comes the reply, "and I don't know whether I should bargain with him until he sells it to me for half price or wait until dark and steal it."

She: "I'll have you know I'm saving myself for marriage."
He: "O.K. After you're married give me a call."

When a husband brings his wife flowers for no reason...
-There is a reason!

Joe is strolling on the beach when suddenly he sees a man, waving and screaming for help, way out there in the water. Joe dives into the surf and manages to save him. After the wizard recovers he turns to Joe and says: "I'm the great wizard Wizmouse, and in gratitude for saving me, I grant you three wishes."

"I want a million dollars," says Joe.

"You'll find the money in your bank account, when you return," answers the wizard.

"I want a magnificent mansion," continues Joe.

"You will find a glorious mansion in place of your old house," promises the wizard. "Anything else?"

"Yes, I want one hundred women."

"Absolutely no problem," says the wizard, "you will find them waiting for you in your mansion. And now, do you mind if I fuck you?"

Joe, totally mesmerized with the wonderful gifts, agrees.

The wizard gets on with it, and when he's finished, asks Joe how old he is.

"Thirty five," replies Joe.

"At your age, you still believe in wizards?"

A man hands his wife an aspirin.
"What's this?"
"An aspirin for your headache."
"But I don't have a headache."
"Gotcha!"

Would you make love with me?
No, but I do appreciate your taste.

Bob goes to his buddy's house where the wife serves an amazing dinner.
"Wow, is he lucky, he's got a gorgeous wife who's also a great cook," sighs Bob.
"Thank you," says the wife, "but I must worn you that Joe is coming home in an hour."
"But I didn't do anything," says Bob, a little surprised.
"I know," replies the wife, "I'm only letting you know how much time you have left..."

A Polack calls a travel agency. "Could you tell me how long it takes to fly to France?"
"One moment, sir..."
"Thank you."

Two friends go to the movies. All of a sudden, one whispers to the other, "I think we'd better move. The guy in the seat next to mine hasn't stopped jerking off since the movie started."
"Well then, let's move," agrees the other.
"But we can't, " she replies.
"Why not?" asks the friend.
"He's using my hand."

What type of fish is always high?
Smoked salmon.

On her birthday, Jacko surprised his mother-in-law with a delicately scented, beautifully wrapped present with a flower and red ribbon.
"Well, Jacko, this is certainly a surprise!" beamed his mother-in-law, "let's see what it is." And she opened the present. In the box she found a pair of beautiful pearl earrings and a pistol.
"These are really lovely, Jacko," she exclaimed, "but why the gun?"
"Oh, that," came the reply, "that's to pierce your ears with."